RealityPoetry Ark Of Inspirational Wisdom

MR. BIGMANN Grier

RealityPoetry Ark of Inspirational Wisdom.

Mr.bigmann@griermediagroup.com

Facebook: Grier Media Group / MrBigmann Grier

Instagram: mr.bigmann_grier

Twitter: @GrierMediaGroup

ISBN-10: 0-9983343-1-6

ISBN-13: 978-0-9983343-1-8

Library of Congress Control Number: 2017910277
Grier Media Group, Macon, GA

Dedicated to those who will take heed and be inspired by truth, wisdom and understanding in order to take personal initiative towards a positive progression in life.

"Allow the inspirational wisdom of RealityPoetry Ark to empower you to aspire with personal initiative. May the realitypoetry written by MR. BIGMANN Grier allow you to bring to light how you've been inspired through the noble wisdom of reality-inspiration and the reputation of morale to aspire for yourself!"

-MR. BIGMANN Grier

CONTENTS

Part VI: Positive-Wisdom

ABOUT THE AUTHOR

Make It Happen

He's far from scared of living life;

His life odyssey of aspirations

And reality inspiration is

His stand at the pulpit!

He confidently gives thanks to

God for exalting his now

Righteous Loccish life!

Unwavering courage and undying faith,

He is one of God's warriors.

His achieving present excels,

Thriving, his future is great!

He has taken progressive responsibility

For his life's fate!

His righteous transition positively glistens,

As the brightest optimistic star.

Who would ever think a stone cold Gangster

Could devour his disputing wrath?

Persistently MR. BIGMANN himself,

A Gangsterman who was never

Afraid of danger.

He's an apex of self-control and innovation,

With determined plans to grow and

Accomplish just as a ripe fruit.

Understanding dollar amounts from cents;

His financially intelligent spirit

Wisely transacts wealth.

His gratifying personality fortifies keen sense,

Mastering a winner attitude,

He never quits!

MR. BIGMANN will never lose consciousness

Of B.G. Lil Trigg (L.I.P) encouraging him...

"Make it happen Bigg homie-

You're always making things happen!"

MR. BIGMANN Grier encourages you,

Who is reading these inspiring words

To take personal initiative for your life

By employing faithful passion-

Help fuel your life!

Make faith your motivation upon your journey.

We all have a purposeful path in life,

Have a determined aim backed by

A strong desire for fulfillment of your purpose.

Keep your mind closed of all negative,

Discouraging and distractive influences.

Cease from being a good

Starter and poor finisher!

Finish what you have started-

Aspire towards making it happen!

The pursuit of perseverance-

Makes things happen!

MR. BIGMANN'S artistic genius within his RealityPoetry of RealityInspiration is the essence of MR. BIGMANN Grier.

RealityPoetry INTRODUCTION

RealityPoetry Wise Reign

The greatest inspirational idea from a wise *RealityPoet* was to write his inspiring and poetic reality-thoughts down. *RealityPoetry* artistry comes alive with the grandest literature reigning laureate sounds. MR. BIGMANN Grier, the wise *RealityPoet* inspires wisdom and minds to thrive. MR. BIGMANN Grier's reality history permeates crafty, profound poetry from undergoing gangland vigorous ties, exerts an assertive, *gangsterous* phraseology drive. The *RealityPoetry* Ark of Inspirational Wisdom Innovates a reality-literary strive. For a wise man conjoins inspiring words, within an inspirational subject of *RealityPoetry-* Aspiring-Wisdom, Fortifying-Wisdom, Street-Wisdom, Spiritual-Wisdom, Love-Wisdom and Positive-Wisdom. MR. BIGMANN Grier inspires poetic insight, creating inspirational, purposeful solutions, impelling an articulate wisdom of *RealityPoetry.* The *RealityPoetry Ark of Inspirational Wisdom,* maintains a wise reign to resolve; from poetically painting inspirational pictures of life and drafting a masterpiece of reality. This balance of moral strength is an inspirational creation of *RealityPoetry* wisdom.

RealityPhorism Sages:

Sayings of wise, inspirational principles and advice for enduring life.

PART I:

ASPIRING-WISDOM

RealityPhorism Sage

Life is a mysterious puzzle. Our reality magnifies in dreams. We inspire to aspire, creating an art of life. We must live to complete an alive Masterpiece.

Chapter 1

No Plans

No plans for life is not living,

It is a confirmation of dying alive.

You need plans to conquer in life;

For a great plan executed

Supports your thrive.

What are your ideas of an ideal life?

No matter your dream

It requires a structured plan;

A strategical plan can be

A victorious scheme.

Therefore, map out your desired plan.

Undergoing the process of your plan

Will induce you towards a fruitful tree.

Nothing in life is subjugated without a plan.

Transcribing your plans are free;

Put in work with faith to be

RealityPoetry Ark of Inspirational Wisdom
MR. BIGMANN GRIER

More than you thought to ever be.

The pursuit of success can beget distress;

Yet, continue your course through struggle.

Persistence marinated ambitiously fuels plans to

Excel beyond the top of any mountain.

For self-discipline keeps you focused.

You are dealing the cards, playing your own hand.

Forever aspire positively disregard negativity.

The one without plans never triumphantly stands.

The future before you is far greater than your past;

For fulfilling your purpose begins with a plan.

Chapter 2

Apply Yourself

(Self-Made)

From positively applying yourself within

Your mind and heart's self-searching,

You will self-destruct your

Self-annihilating negativity by

Self-starting yourself forward with positivity.

Self-sowing righteousness more

Than yesterday's negativity.

Self-determination will morph self-assertion.

Being self-mastered won't let anything

Stop your self-preservation.

Absorbing self-realization self-ordains

Your self-worth, so excuse your self-abuse

Of degrading self-expressions.

Apply yourself, loving self.

Self-love is not to self-abandon.

It is evident you will triumphantly self-fulfill

Your dreams by having self-control;

With progressive self-esteem.

Fortifying your self-will regulates

Your self-confidence; your vision is

Self-inspired by your dreams.

Productively, self-employ your self-serving;

You will successfully satisfy yourself.

Forget not the love of God;

Sacrifice yourself with self-devotion.

You'll never be limited when

Walking as a self-reflection of God!

For faith and blessful deeds are

Blessed from the one who applies

Himself to give life itself!

Thanks is being selfless not selfish.

Applying a self-analysis of self-righteousness,

Keeps you from being self-centered.

Applying self-sufficiency with self-study

Keeps you self-tolerant.

Applying self-suggestion will build

Powerful character within yourself.

Your self-importance relies on optimistic

Self-assurance; being self-same

Is your self-evidence.

Applying poised positivity you

Will have self-made yourself.

Chapter 3

Think Big

Be wise enough to think big.

Envision big visions, thinking big!

Inspire your thoughts to think big.

The bigger your dream-

The bigger your reality will become!

Think big empowering your means;

Big eminence begets big thinking.

Being big-hearted with big-money

Proves you're in the big-league.

Thinking big creates big-business.

Have big-integrity when conducting business;

A big-lie will make you unworthy of belief.

You can close big-deals in life when thinking big.

Be the big-enchilada with an

Ambition to achieve.

Think of big-progress with everything you do.

With big-expansion and big-efficiency

In all you do!

Think big-ideas to construct bigger

Opportunities and purpose within your life.

Thinking big comes with big-reputation;

It is great to have big-dedication.

Thinking big is growth worthy;

From exercising big-thoughts

You will motivate extraordinarily.

There is big-magic in thinking big;

Your life will interchange magnificently.

A wise thinker will master big-thinking.

Chapter 4

Envision your Vision

Look within the blessings in your vision;

For the provision you see is your victory.

Therefore, your life is seen through-

The life you envision!

Do not view your life as a mysterious collision.

Acknowledge your vision;

Put forth effort towards accomplishing your vision!

What is foreseen are the dreams you envisioned!

The actuality seen is the reality of your dream.

Fail at holding yourself back and

Prevail begetting your vision-facts.

What you envision relies upon your active decision.

Have discernment of your vision;

You are seeing within the mind's eye.

In life, divination is visual through our imagination!

We can bring alive anything envisioned;

From employing our creative imagination.

Take heed to the keenness of

This wise *RealityPoetry* insight;

Your foreknowledge can't be learned in college.

We all have the faculty of sight

Which begets revelations of our life;

Therefore, a vivid vision is one

Of the greatest ideas envisioned!

Realize with persistence- your vision!

Chapter 5

Educated Rider

Balance is an accuracy with education,

When riding off the fuel of intelligence.

Think accomplished thoughts;

Achieving significant knowledge.

Learning encourages growth within life;

Having common sense keeps you from

Thinking twice or thrice.

A keen mindset always invigorates life;

Through finances, academics, profession and health.

Uneducated of either unbalances life.

For without academic education,

Your ability to read and write is an-

Academic *illiteracation*!

For without professional education,

Your skills are ignorant.

For without health education,

You will become ill.

Nevertheless, experiences of

Life excels your education.

Riding of the knowledge from education

Gives your life more life to live!

Great education expands your mindset.

Exercise your goals to proceed in

Obtaining knowledge to succeed.

Ride with an education,

Drive through life towards success.

Love to learn, reach never-heights;

Learn to love educating your life!

For an educated rider,

Forever educates their life...

Chapter 6

You are Somebody

Even if you think you are a *Nobody*

You are always *Somebody.*

For a Nobody is still a *Somebody,*

So realize You are *Somebody*!

No matter what is said by *Anybody,*

You are within the world amongst *Everybody*.

And if perceived as a *Nobody,*

Take the personal initiative to be *Somebody*.

You are *Somebody!*

Not that perception of a *Nobody*!

Everybody should always see themselves

Optimistically as *Somebody.*

So then, the *Nobody*, pessimistic hate can't

Stimulate depress in *Anybody.*

We are all *Somebody!*

Look in the mirror and say-

"I am Somebody!"

Well, who are you now as Somebody?

Define yourself with positive embody.

The truth is, you have always been *Somebody*.

You simply had to exit the negatively

Perceived shell of a *Nobody.*

Now walk confidently into the world

To win you *Somebody!*

Find a good friend or mate

For *Everybody* is *Somebody!*

Chapter 7

Good Hearts

For everyone claims they are good;

But do you have a good heart?

Good faith inspires good hearts;

Become compassionate within your heart.

Love others as you desire to be loved.

Good will is a good nature never to depart;

For it is not wise to say goodbye to goodness!

Good humor brings sunshine-smiles in life.

Acquire good fellowship with good people.

Within an obedient matrimony,

A good man will honor a good wife;

No one desires a good for nothing life.

Follow the good books instructions,

It's a good study for a good heart.

Every day is a Good Friday when

Your heart beats a good temper!

God blesses a faithful good heart.

Keep your health intact,

For good health maintains a

Good looking good heart.

Good minds together produce

Positively good facts;

Value good thoughts worthy of

Good hearted transactions.

Live for the good.

Life can be gracefully good.

Having a good heart is attractive,

Confident, genuine, kind,

Loyal, positive and obedient!

To possess a good heart is good;

If you don't own a good heart

Now is a good time to acquire one!

Chapter 8

Take the Risk

Life's progression is full of risk;

To proceed- take the risk.

Along all roads there will be many

Decisions to be made-

Decide to take the risk!

You will only stop your growth when

Being precautious to soar-

Spread your wings and take the risk!

Be proactive and you will excel.

You live once but may die plenty of times;

By stagnating your life with fear-

Overcome fears and take the risk!

Failing does not make you a failure;

Let it motivate you to try again-

Fortune begets from taking the risk!

Taking the risk doesn't count your strikes;

It pushes you to hit successful runs-

With a confident swing take the risk!

You can't control the might of every wind;

But you can take the risk and win.

Take the risk and become a winner!

The world revolves with risks taken daily.

Do not be afraid;

Make your risk worth your benefit.

The RealityPoet MR. BIGMANN Grier took a risk-
Composing inspiration; for art becomes reality!

Chapter 9

Impurities reformed Purifies

Finding your other self-

Intentionally comes when in crisis.

Living has greater efficiency when you

Begin to know thy self!

Life is lived morally by allowing

Positivity to dwell within you and

Rejecting immoral negativity.

Finding peace through God brings

Peace, peacefully within self.

Thinking right empowers living righteously.

You can't think wrong and purify yourself;

Think right and be righteous.

Refurbished impurities purify self;

It comes with breaking an

Impure mold and cleansing yourself.

Chance is the perception of "*if*";

Therefore, don't engage in impurity's myth.

Faith is the law that purifies life.

By faith the world we live was created-

Not from *"what if"!*

Take control of your life dwelling in faith.

Resolve fear with faith;

Renovate hate with love;

Replace anger with peace;

Redeem insecurity with confidence;

Renew weakness with strength;

Refrain from impure influences;

Reawaken your life with purities.

A refreshed life inspires reformed purification.

Chapter 10

Wrong Direction Correction

Walking the directed "Journey of Broke" is

In the direction of a wrong job!

Living 'Just over broke' is

Having a No-purpose drive!

If this is your life you're living dead,

No motivation or determined purpose to strive.

Fuel your talents to accomplish in life;

Focus your goals until they are successfully alive!

Prudently watch who you follow in life;

Majority neglect to achieve living in life.

Excuse talk of negative faith,

Which are just emotions from a hate-fate.

Many are afraid of risk,

Therefore playing everything safe.

These are steps of fearing mistakes.

The ones who succeed are individuals

Who don't live to procrastinate.

There will always be a "*what if...*"

Or "*you can't...*" stop sign;

In the mind and heart that can't success relate!

Chart your course to victoriously excel even

If you drive through failure.

Failing forward is a lesson learned.

The direction you choose will

Direct your livelihood into reality.

Your life is chosen!

You only have one life to live.

Be productive and fortunately gain;

Directing your life with nothing to lose.

Drive to successfully thrive!

Chapter 11

Stop Proving and Start Improving

Channel your strength excelling to win

Towards an excellency of longevity.

Always keep your mind free of nonsense;

Employ common sense-it makes sense!

It will help you sum up financial Cents in the process!

Be as you were born- free!

Are you not independent?

Live successfully, improving your reality!

Secure positivity by improving yourself first.

Repress negativity, struggling is a

Trial that can be surpassed.

In reality it takes genuine effort

For a tribulation not to last.

The reality-truth may hurt;

Yet it is best to execute productivity and

Trust your improving will to work.

Let it workout the pessimistic

Problems within your life!

Procrastinating can prove to be

Cancerous to your life's fate.

Progress proving you are great!

Proving to yourself- you can improve yourself!

Chapter 12

Take Action

Don't rigid yourself waiting purposely;

Being patient with hesitation;

Subject to an appealing devastation

That comes from the contact sport

Called procrastination!

We live in a country of multi-mixed fruits,

A culture of different races with

Differentiations of living variations.

Still we live within the same places,

Many bodies of one nation.

No matter religion or faith;

We are all made of one creation.

Instilled with purpose;

We can all inspire life with triumph.

What is your purpose in living?

Seek it courageously while living;

Establish your life's attitude with Godspeed.

Blind faith will make your life fruitfully breed!

Conquer the mountain with great ease;

Take action challenging yourself in life,

For living is your grand opponent.

There is no great comfort in stagnation.

Fear nothing in living your life.

Take action- opportunity is yours!

Take action- victory is yours!

PART II:

FORTIFYING –WISDOM

Chapter 13

Feed Us!

Can we have something to eat?

Feed our minds a keen education;

So that we can become knowledgeable.

Feed our poor minds-

Feed us higher education!

Can we have something to eat?

Feed our bodies rich nutrients;

So that we can endure for a life time.

Feed our poor bodies-

Feed us nutritious health!

Can we have something to eat?

Feed us opportunities;

So that we can stand on our feet.

Poverty stricken has us homeless on the streets.

Feed our poor living-

Feed us with great opportunities!

Can we have something to eat?

Feed our hearts with moral love;

So that we don't digest dishonesty and hate.

Feed our poor love-

Feed us with fortifying love!

Can we have something to eat?

Feed our communities with development;

So that our playgrounds have a future.

Feed our poor communities-

Feed us by reviving our communities!

Can we have something to eat?

Feed us fairness in the criminal justice system;

So that we are not obese with penal injustice.

Feed our poor justice-

Feed us with fair justice!

Can we have something to eat?

Feed our spirits with divinity;

So that God's grace inspires more faith.

Feed our poor spirits-

Feed us with God-speed and spirituality!

Chapter 14

Yesterday Expired Inspiring Today's Hope

Yesterday expired yesterday;

It will never come back.

Live hopefully inspired in the now;

For today is where your hopes are.

Disown dwelling in yesterday's impassioned past.

Forgive today or else yesterday lives on.

Yesterday did not inspire a present hope to surpass;

No matter what yesterday suffered tomorrow's

Hope will not hold that sorrow.

Absorb a hopeful inspirational energy of now;

Confidence today will show you how.

Yesterday's expiration balances hope inspirations.

Today's manhood expires yesterday's boyhood;

Today's joy expires yesterday's pain;

Today's womanhood expires yesterday's girlhood.

Yesterday's loss invigorates today's gain;

Yesterday's plight inspires today's might.

Today's morning expired yesterday's night.

Overcome yesterday today;

For another experience is optimistically on its way!

Dismiss leaning on yesterday's expired times;

Let God be your inspiring hope-

Faithfully all the time!

Chapter 15

Power

The world is on a drug known as

Power!

The first drug with a drug's high-

Power!

Nation to nation we fight for-

Power!

Money begets a value with-

Power!

Respect is respective of-

Power!

We all are friends for-

Power!

Life is devoured by-

Power!

We live to obtain-

Power!

There is strength in-

Power!

Some behold and then abuse-

Power!

Only to be destroyed by-

Power!

If you gain power-

How will you handle power?

Do you think you can tame power?

Can you maintain power?

Look within your heart and mind;

Only you can discover your power;

When you find it stay in control of your power;

Be not afraid of life's power;

Make a difference with your power;

For power can conquest power!

Balance living positively Powerful!

Chapter 16

Today's Adversity begets Tomorrow's Sunshine

As the moon does not hide from the night;

Be not afraid of life's untimely plight.

The snow's hail may have come from hard rain;

Dare not let the storm take your rebuilding might.

Today's adversity begets tomorrow's sunshine.

The flood may have washed properties away.

To overcome- strength must prevail,

As life restores to live for another day.

Today's adversity begets tomorrow's sunshine.

When mother-nature endures labor,

The earth feels her wrath.

Let your tears be your effort to

Reconstruct and ambitiously excel.

For adversity is where sunshine avails.

Today's adversity begets tomorrow's sunshine.

From Mother Nature's birth force

A super storm can take course.

The misfortune of this fate can

Beget love from cities and states.

Aiding one another will be the sun shining great;

Support your neighbor through today's adversity.

Today's adversity begets tomorrow's sunshine.

Devote a moment of silence-

For the lives that traveled to a heavenly home;

Pray faithfully and never mourn materials lost,

Possessions can be regained again.

Enjoy your survival of life with

Respect for the neighbors lost;

For their joy and dreams are with the wind.

Today's adversity begets tomorrow's sunshine.

We discover life each day we awaken;

Exploring death each night we sleep.

With life's heartbeat adverse emotions

Are defeated by sunshine.

In any circumstance of adversity,

Sunshine reconditions life to be complete.

Today's adversity begets tomorrow's sunshine.

Today's adversity begets tomorrow's sunshine.

**Dedicated to the family and victims of Hurricane Sandy ... 2012*

Chapter 17

Confident Manhood

From dust matter of the earth-

God molded into creation man.

Man's will is to live bountifully

Over his given turf!

A man of God manfully manifolds manhood.

The man is bred to conquer;

And be persistent daily in life!

Manhood courage is an essential at heart.

The art of embodying No fear lives within.

I, MR. BIGMANN Grier am a man;

You are a man, he is a man, we are men!

We were made to be free,

With an independent manhood.

For it is a man's world;

With men reigning since genesis.

Real men optimize their manhood;

Defining a manic status quo.

Whether *Gangstermen*, businessmen or gentlemen-

All are the staunch boldness of manhood.

Will power is man-sized within grown men;

Man power is confident in manhood.

A man shall possess manners for a woman.

Between the sheets mannish manhood comes alive;

With mandingo manhandling the vulva.

Manly testosterone loves the

Estrogen within womanhood!

For a Kingsman's manhood lives majestically;

Forever managing as the man of the house.

Being a great dad to man's child real men provide

Love so their sons and daughters hearts smile.

Men of war manhunt in manmade betrayal;

Disloyalty is not found in authentic manhood.

Man is a creation that creates himself by

Taking charge with purposeful responsibilities.

This is the mantic of manhood!

Chapter 18

Strong Womanhood

Women, you are never a bitch;

No matter how much emphasis or over-hearing;

Or if invigorated from your spiteful actions.

Woman-to-woman refrain from

Calling one another a bitch;

For no man wants to be the son of a bitch!

Degrading self will initiate someone else to

Chant out the same disheartening pitch.

Women, not only are you beauty;

You are strength and rich.

Never mind what despised hate inoculates;

Continue to hold your head high.

Women, there are men who understand your pain.

MR. BIGMANN Grier is one of many real men;

So let a real man help soothe your distress!

How could any real man hate a strong woman?

When man was conceived and

Nurtured by the love of a woman.

Men, fortify your woman.

Women, accept the fortification of man's love.

We must stop undermining the power

Of woman's loving strength.

Forgive us women for we are

Blinded by our manly authority.

Women, you break the mold of frail inferiority.

Women of the world, recognize your

Ambitious strength as in a mirror.

You will overcome any burden with

Faithful strength in God for certain.

Women, motherhood can have heartfelt pain

When not godly understood.

Don't diverge from your motherly strength of love;

Neglecting the love needing hearts of your children.

Despite the fact that your womanhood may have

Underwent bitter years of struggle from-

Molestation stress, childhood love negligence,

Battered tears distress, scars of belittling,

Poverty stricken burdens, rape, oppression,

Broken-hearted love and confused emotional anger.

Mighty woman, never forget God loves you!

Women, strongly love yourself and think positive

From the confident heart within;

For the strength within your spirit is alive.

**This reality-poem is MR. BIGMANN Grier's way of inspirationally motivating your strong will; so that you may aspire to living successfully- thriving! Women, take a strong stand in positively, peacefully and prosperously expanding. You are the piece created within God's plan to fellowship with man. You are more than capable within your strong womanhood to aspire and expand. Believe in your will and acknowledge the strength within your heart.*

Chapter 19

Motherhood

"She watches over the ways of her household and does not eat the bread of idleness."

Forevermore, mothers bear the birth of life;

Nurturing motherhood's love within her womb.

From the beginning to the dawn a

Mother's love consumes.

This sacred love of motherhood devotes;

Love of God, love of virtue and love of children.

Motherly love is never given in vain.

Strong motherhood vitally possess love

To guide a child's heart out of the distress rain.

For this is part of the magnificent love

Your divine motherhood contains.

Motherhood is the reason every child

Cries for their mother when in pain!

Even when under stress your love

Continues to motherhood manifest.

The greatest motherhood quote expressed;

"A mother knows best"

No son, daughter or grandchild can

Detest motherly love expressed.

Know that your motherhood is appreciated.

Today and tomorrow may your

Motherhood be blessed!

For every day is a mother's day!

Chapter 20

Fatherhood Love

For the third Sunday in June is

The day we honor father's love!

However, fatherhood love is loving every day;

From the one who is a father figure everyday.

For as a man is, so is his love's strength.

A father's love empowers-

Fatherhood's love strength!

Fathom a child without fatherhood love...

A lonely heart that is yearning

A satisfying fatherhood love.

Fatherhood love is a virtuous gift from

The heavenly God above.

All fathers must give strong love;

Let God's love be our prototype.

Fatherhood devotion must endure a consistent

Benevolence of love.

If you never felt any paternal

Guidance of fatherhood love;

Let not your fatherly affection keep in absence;

For you know the feeling of fatherless love.

Motherhood needs more fatherhood support.

Refrain from letting a child suffer non-support;

And being labeled a good-for-nothing

In child support court.

Keep your fatherhood love loving and

Never let your love abort.

For a great father always provides

A loving fatherhood love support!

Chapter 21

Never Too...

You're never too low to stand;

Never too low to withstand.

You're never too down to give up;

Never too down to get up.

You're never too hurt to heal;

Never too numb to feel.

You're never too wicked to be kind;

Never too broke to financially incline.

You're never too smart to learn;

Never too ignorant to knowledge earn

You're never too dumb to be wise;

Never too closed-minded to open-mind rise.

You're never too hateful to love;

Never too hopeless to hope.

You're never too dishonest to be truthful;

Never too discouraged to be encouraged.

Never too discouraged to be encouraged.

You're never too doubtful to believe;

Never too weak to be strong.

You're never too wrong to be right;

Never too pagan to be righteous.

Chapter 22

Altering an Evil Ego

(Evil Eviction)

From wunderkind interchanging times to

Undergoing delinquent adolescent plight;

Your young ambitious hearts are not evil.

Experiencing ages of indiscretion can overcome

Struggling nights in an age of ignorance.

Dare not let egos of evil stereotypes blind

Your rising generation's mind.

Alter your awkward age's evil

Ego form dominating pain.

Your tender age heart has to stand strong;

You will witness the power.

Feed yourself with daily positive bread;

As you aim and gramercy God every day.

Excel upon enacting progressive fame;

If you've undergone tough childhood pain.

Know in heart strength and thriving;

After the hailing rain with productive striving-

The sunshine reigns.

Expel evil thoughts from your growing mind;

Eviscerate the exceptional negative evil eye.

You will evolve Reconstructing an evil mind.

Mature, excavating evil doing;

Stop your evil ruining by exalting successful growth.

For God continuously blesses the child-

That vigorously holds their own!

Transcend from making the younger

Generation's life bleed;

A step towards the next generation's correction,

Despite all the evil activity enacted-

Take heed!

For more early adulthood direction,

God is ready to successfully direct.

Don't give up on a new fledged life by

Walking with evil.

You can cry violently or silently in strife;

Let prayer give you strength;

May you undergo better sleeping nights.

MR. BIGMANN Grier is a bellwether who wisely

Understands your evil evicting fight;

Due to an evil ego he once had as

A youngster with might.

He is evidence of an altered evil ego;

An evil eviction from the

Lessons in life's plight.

Trust, it can be a hard fight.

Imagine your youth captured with penal life;

Or a missing memory of life on a t-shirt…

Fathom your desires for your future life;

Claim victory and positively live;

Overstand the evicting of an evil ego to support

Excelling in a life you freely live!

Invest in adulthood with respect for your future.

Faith, virtue, knowledge, self-control,

Perseverance, peace of mind and heart;

Brotherly kindness and love will

Help evict your evil ties!

Look pass the negative hype that you're

Living to die!

Envision your future;

Living fruitfully and surpassing all evil lies...

**Understand when knowledge becomes dangerous and voices of truth are shunned, despised, or silenced; for then ignorance is rewarded.*

Chapter 23

Unequal Freedom

Dollars are collateral for securing freedom;

When you have no cents your freedom

Becomes an unsecured reality-

Unequally not making sense!

A borrowed dollar compounds equaling cents.

Equal opportunities become unequal;

When you lose another one wins.

Freedom is the question unequally defended;

Are the black and white race not equal?

Are blacks and Hispanics an equal minority?

Will the answers be easy to comprehend?

The answer is poverty, poverty creates inequality.

Overcrowded prisons with blacks and Hispanics;

Dreams encaged, a product of privileged,

Unjust interest schemes.

Can you hear the screams for freedom and justice?

Today we are smoke screened to the inequality.

Are women equal to man?

Are we all an equal body of humans?

Are we divided by good and evil?

Poor and rich? Positive and negative?

Life is an equal to death.

What do life's free breaths equal?

The air we breathe is gives freedom;

And with it the strength and equal right to live.

Healthcare is another unequal debate.

Sickness deserves free healing.

Love didn't know hate until

Equality got mad at freedom's fate.

We must learn to equally resolve and

Live life freely to evolve.

In genius mind, equality involves

Thoughts of freedom and free will.

Greed will give a line of credit to

Equality and then withdraw it

So that freedom can't pay.

Freedom shall be debt free,

Equality shall be priceless;

When the valuation of equality becomes costless.

Chapter 24

Fake Free

Excuse yourself of fake men whose

Lie-abilities are real.

Exalt yourself with genuine men whose

Truth-assets are real.

Authenticity dares not vouch for fake men;

Yet many are feigns to the characteristic of sin.

Life is too real to live fake!

Be Alive in your life,

Experience it free of fake.

Living within lies is a prevailing death!

The *RealityPoet* transcribing this *realitypoem*

Is way too real to not tell a realty-truth!

MR. BIGMANN prescinds the fake from the real;

With a presence of mind too solid to refute.

His prestige is far from fraudulent;

He's actual and factual with an

Unmasked originality!

The world is overcrowded with falsehood intents;

With fake pretense from woman and man.

When the elements of someone's heartbeats

Are not true, *who can you trust?*

Truth-lies, do they lie within you?

Thou shall never fake *kick it;*

No matter how fake someone may be;

Forever be true to yourself and that

Is the personal initiative to being *fake-free*!

Refurbish your life and dissipate bogus people.

Take this literal fortification upon

Your life to be fake-free;

Continue to be real with self,

Him, her and we!

Chapter 25

Only Peace Solely Loves

Peace loves the world.

Love, loves to be peaceful.

If only the world loved peace;

The world would be at peace and full of love.

Serenity has no love for war;

War lives to despise peace.

If only we could live in harmony;

All the world's wars would cease.

Solely, let our loving hearts

Come alive with peace,

And our heartbeat's love increase.

Violence will only surrender to peace.

It will take our love- for war to decease.

We all have a life that will

Come to rest in peace;

So while living give love

And live within peace.

Love never hates and peace is never angry.

Peace loves unity and unity loves peace.

Solely, love everyday so war will cease.

For peace solely loves;

And love solely makes peace.

For peace solely loves;

And love solely makes peace.

For peace solely loves;

And love solely makes peace.

Chapter 26

The Face of Revelations

When a man cannot motivate his heartbeat,

He cheats the life he has to live.

Restrained breathing is a life unworthy to live!

Envisioning beyond the everyday life seen,

Supports accomplishing life's reality-dream.

There shouldn't be a feeling of living scared;

Gain experience from living so you may move ahead.

Life's eloquent strife is not to dread;

For it is an experience in life.

Life itself encounters all living struggles.

O, the feeling when man accepts life's affection,

For the face of revelations can't be lost.

Every day is a yesterday,

As tomorrow is a today.

To overstand what a life may face,

Life can only understand-

By living to face!

Facing the reality which life lives to create.

The creator gave his creation sovereignty in life,

To incline thoughts within the mind,

To be dimensional, to think for self-

A universal divine!

Life while living is one of a kind.

Once life is no more- living becomes blind!

This revelation was designed way before

Existence in any lifetime.

Enjoy life by living on a progressive incline.

Behold life and live successfully,

Accept the alive passion of every second.

No matter the situation- overcome by living.

Life's reality will live through the ages,

Own no age, for in life you are never too old to live.

Chapter 27

Trigger Intellect

Triggering immaculate thoughts of intellectualism,

My integrity of insurrection is more than intense.

I question the reasons-

Why educators are under-valued and

Schools attendance is low due to an

Integration of our youth to the streets?!

MR. BIGMANN Grier inspirits inevitable victory;

With positive, prosperous intellect he

Advocates for youngsters,

Interceding love over hate.

Forget not God's rule- to not youth despise!

Discipline with corrections of love and

Make them opulently rise.

Look into his eyes to see his heart.

The intellectual righteous intentions of

The infamous MR. BIGMANN Grier is to

Trigger the intellect of courageous minds.

Call it *intellect hustling-*

The fortifying of an intellectual grind.

The truth will be far from ill advised;

As inexperienced mentalities interact,

Experiencing intellectual potentiality!

The steel curtain of ineffective thoughts will fall,

Unveiling life with abundant competence.

With the mind not being dumbed down,

Knowing how to think in life will be certain.

Dreams successfully become reality;

New thoughts are a new age of successful incline.

An indwelling intellect for the

New generation of mighty minds!

Living out goals is not hard when

Accomplishing is in mind and

Your visions are not fearful.

Inspire yourself to think beyond today;

Your tomorrow's future will not be hard to find.

Death finds everyone in life;

Don't let it find you while-

Not living to exceed.

Greatly feed your intellect –

The creative food it needs!

Chapter 28

Un-depress your Stress

You will not make everyone happy.

Yet, continue to make *you*r heart happy

By exerting happy love.

Don't congest your joy with agony.

Un-depress yourself by being happy-

Happy that you're alive!

With worry, stress kills life.

Depressing yourself is living unhealthy.

Faith will strengthen life to overcome.

Un-depress yourself and you will prevail.

Depression makes thinking fail,

And stress pushes happiness to hell.

Empower your wellbeing internally,

And you'll destroy stress unwanted hell.

The way you feel at heart is always revealed.

Think not what you can't do,

Think about doing what you can do.

Stress happiness and joy for yourself and others.

Stressing love is what is good for your health.

Don't let life's pressures stress you;

Take control by being joyous.

Un-depress your stress, always love yourself.

Chapter 29

Humility doesn't Humiliate

Meekness doesn't humiliate humility.

In truth, humbleness isn't fortuitous.

Being modest is fortified by humility;

Humiliation disrespects humbleness

By harming a calm spirit.

Don't degrade your character praising hostility;

Arrogance deducts from your ability.

Pride can be a road to shame;

While humility can free your heart of pride.

Refrain from making a fool of yourself.

Be strong while still being gentle as a lamb.

Hateful thoughts will depress a peaceful mind.

Hatred kills the soul.

Adopt the obedience to optimistically think!

Humility begets from a divine lifeline.

The discomfort of humiliation destroys friendships.

Vain glory is void of humility and kindness.

Embrace humility with natural kinship;

Allow it to lead with honor and wisdom.

For humble advice will induce your life.

Chapter 30

Do You Really?

Do you really feel me?

Awakening in a concrete one man cell,

Caged in behind a steel door 24 hours a day.

Do you really feel me?

Fighting the devil with God's grace.

Do you really feel me?

Reminiscing of wiping Love's brains off your face.

Do you really feel me?

Reading letters from your G-Ma,

Hoping she's still alive to welcome you home.

Do you really feel me?

Living life for real;

While politicians lie about it- for real!

Do you really feel me?

Pen in hand, inscribing reality thoughts.

Do you really feel me?

Exerting positivity- hard

In order to mind-eyes of the blind!

Do you really feel me?

Wanting to exhale blunt smoke in order to cope;

But instead inhaling breaths of hope.

Do you really feel me?

Conquering hate and

Victoriously enjoying peace within.

Do you really feel me?

Exiting negative darkness into an optimistic light.

Do you really feel me?

Educating yourself with financial literacy,

Expertise and businessman savvy.

Do you really feel me?

Delegating in business despite penal-absence.

Do you really feel me?

Attempting to deal with a pessimistic woman,

Not recognizing a good man and forward progress.

Do you really feel me?

Never giving up or falling

Into failure's pit of distress.

Do you really feel me?

With sons awaiting a home arrival;

Asking when? As their love is expressed.

Do you really feel me?

Mind focused, envisioning a life victory!

Do you really feel me?

Everyone says they feel me!

Do you really feel me?

Do you really?

You feel me?

Chapter 31

Express Yourself

Finding a way to express yourself-

Can be mean!

Finger pointing at the youth is

An expression of your *no love* means.

Don't just express opinions of what needs to stop;

First, stop being a critic, you're helping not!

The youth have inherited expressing themselves

With the clip and the trigger.

Not because they intentionally wanted to;

But maybe due to it being how the

World expresses itself too.

Life in front of them shows pain through violence;

Relieving life's stresses with that expression.

Finding constructive methods for youngsters,

To express positively, grow and learn.

Expression makes an impression;

Whether good or bad.

If your opportunities are greater than

The next man then grant them

The opportunity to stand;

Expressing a helping hand and

Acknowledging wisdom.

PART III

STREET-WISDOM

Chapter 32

Fear Not

For I am not a Free-Mason.

Yet, I know society's secrets.

I am a free thinker!

MR. BIGMANN Grier has cognizance of

The American stock within the real streets,

Riding high loccish deep, tough as sin.

For beats pound gang-bang hard,

The truth reveals every heart is not solid.

Thus, living is a life lesson learned.

For we make friends solely

To turn them into enemies.

Foes hate attempts to assassinate-

The respect earned from a maturing discerned!

When money becomes your truest homie,

You will be acknowledged as changed,

As you splurge with your rich monetary friend.

When one has lost their strive-

They expect you not to productively thrive.

One great prayer a day will bring victory alive.

Laziness is never an ambitious way

To fuel life on a prosperous drive.

Scandalous women lust to come upon a winner;

For a winner lust to thrive.

There are no exceptions to a distraction

Upon a triumphant mission;

Focus is the persistence of

An accomplishing submission.

It is not impossible to do as you desire;

Especially when it comes to achieving

All you could every possibly desire!

Your vision can see- your vision is clear!

All is possible when your motivation doesn't fear.

Fret not! To breathe is not a threat;

For nothing will fail thee when

Your faith knows God is prevailing in thee!

Chapter 33

Guns Down and Fists Up

You can blast with rounds until

Someone murderously goes down;

Man up and put the guns down.

You're missing loved ones now;

From empty clips of gun sounds.

Fists up and fight on the battle ground.

Hope you're not trying to street impress;

The media crucifies suspects in the press!

Fists up is the best way to address conflict;

Guns down so you can box rounds.

Roy Jones Jr., Floyd Mayweather, Mike Tyson-

Knocks out with guns down!

You will live to see another day,

To talk about it and walk around.

We all have families to feed;

Why attempt to make them grieve?

Fists up-

Real men can handle a nose bleed,

Or a swollen face;

But you can't stand a murder case.

Live to see another day.

Guns down-

You don't need an "A.K.";

Allow today to be a good day.

Fists going up to resolve a dispute is

Better than allowing your guns to shoot.

You will live to see another day.

Fists up in a mutual combat;

Can you all handle that?

Don't give the prosecutor an opportunity to indict

On a theorized murder act.

Don't chance your freedom within the eyes of rats.

You can resolve whatever with understanding;

Think about all you're sacrificing and losing

When the gun blasts and you thought you won.

You don't have to quarrel by the gun!

Guns down and fists up!

What's up?

Knuckle up to man up!

Chapter 34

Street Duez (Paid)

In his valor days of old he rode high with

Time-Bomb Loc, Gangsta-Dre (LIP), Bigg Simm,

Killa and *Bigg Pookie Loc (LIP*).

MR.BIGMANN embodies titanium nerves and no fear

From the courageous womb of 3rd Street

To anywhere, swerving in the “Blue Ghost”,

Banging “Crip-Hop” with Loccish *LilMann,*

Q-TIP and *Scrapp Loc*, rip-riding nonstop.

Undergoing multiple blue moons behind the gun.

His hustle energy accounted abundant cash stock,

Thus, he is coming home on an ethical,

Financial money run.

Loccish homies and adversaries confirm-

His esteemed street duez!

He was known to be crip-arrogant,

With an attitude of gangster demand.

RealityPoetry Ark of Inspirational Wisdom
MR. BIGMANN GRIER

Women admired his assertive ways

As he C'walked in his dick-doggs.

His sexual healing inspired climaxful feelings.

No matter wrong or right-

All night he was down to fight.

The street beats within his TrueBlue heart.

Always down to Loccish ride,

For the life he lead was his might.

Respectfully liquor was poured for the

Loccish loved ones "L.I.P" out of sight.

His love extended countywide with money orders

For the Monday and Friday store calls.

His pad accepted every collect call.

Only the 1st generation of loccish riders will recall.

Today he fathoms that,

His flesh is temporary and

God has made his spirit whole!

Today he inspirationally writes *realitypoetry,*

And articulates reality-truth jewels;

Optimistically feeding a fortifying bread

RealityPoetry Ark of Inspirational Wisdom
MR. BIGMANN GRIER

To the young adults and beyond.

MR. BIGMANN's vengeance is God!

His street duez were paid,

Macon no mistakes begetting his

Now righteous revelation!

Thou shall not debase his encouraging heart.

Forevermore he will endow positive

Solutions towards making a difference

Upon all debased hearts.

If you haven't lived the ganglife it's

Hard to understand the debased hearts.

Forevermore his spirit is of God!

Enriching the ride for the urban class,

To drive their life pass the gun,

Around prison and towards-

Avoiding an early grave.

MR. BIGMANN's reality-inspiration are

Jewels of encouraging peace,

Positivity and prosperity.

Chapter 35

Lead Showers

When it rains it pours lead.

A good prayer is needed before

You leave home in the morning.

Everyday and all night it's raining lead.

Lead can have you grieving a homie;

Or your love ones will have you to mourn.

Lead showers will have you dodging for your life.

The streets has no true love!

Yet men love to die by loving

To live within the street life.

Have you ever heard a 44 Magnum

Shot right behind your ear?

Your eardrums ring an echoing song

From the big bang- it's evident no theory!

Can you withstand running

Fast as you can in the rain

Praying no to get wet?

If you do get wet your blood soaked.

Don't get caught up in a hailing lead storm.

A Choke on a blunt won't be your last choke.

In exchange for smoke-

You'll have blood in your throat.

In every inner city and through the nation,

It's about power or the simplistic

Misunderstanding being devoured.

You can be the hardest man or softest coward;

When it rains it pours.

If you're in the streets playing with guns,

It's not easy to escape a lead shower.

Don't get caught in the rain.

When it rains it pours.

Chapter 36

Cease Fire (Making Peace)

For it is visible to you, them and we-

Your flag is blue, your flag is black, your flag is red;

You all can pass by on another

Without a disrespectful word said.

An authentic definition of

Men respecting one another is when

There is no dispute or blood shed.

Neither tribe wants to lose a brother or sister,

Nor leave a homie behind.

The detriment of firing copper lead.

'Stop the violence' Is a sad song preached.

MR. BIGMANN's reality poems is a

Change of heart reached

To cease fire by making peace.

Do you really want to die in these streets?

Your life six feet deep can be an answer;

If you neglect to cease fire in the streets.

Putting down your gun doesn't make a man weak;

The weak has no understanding in

Overcoming destructible beef.

A man that has understandable strength lives

His life enduring positively complete.

If you think everyone is your enemy-

Why not become your own best friend?

You can listen to your other self;

Inform yourself – killing another person isn't a win!

Life in jail awaits that sin.

Making peace is to cease fire my friend.

You can be reputable of your tribe culture positively

And chart your life upon a progressive win.

Being confined justly or unjustly for bangin'

Your tribe against another tribe-

Is the short journey in your life towards its end.

Being locked behind crucifying unjust walls;

You're tricking yourself to be penally pimped.

Prison is a brilliant dollar industry;

Pay attention- plantation to penitentiary!

Cease fire by retiring gun fire.

Look beyond your life of hard-time excuses;

Believe not even in your own excuses!

When behind unjust walls,

All caged together on a prison yard;

The tribes you think you hate

You now live enthralled with.

Yet, you reasonably respect one another

On the prison yard; when free you

Can give the same acknowledgment and regards.

You don't have to enter prison

To respect another tribal culture.

Live your life peacefully,

Live it successfully and

Don't attempt to destroy another life.

Optimistically live and empower your life.

Excel to excellence!

Cease fire and make peace!

Educate yourself and choose to aspire.

Gunfire will not prevail;

It derails and brings demise to living life.

Cease fire, make peace!

Chapter 37

Alive Beyond 25

The hood slangs bullets-

Just as the block slangs rocks!

It's a sport to throw rocks at the penitentiary;

We played this game everyday nonstop.

We're missing encaged loved ones;

For a prison decade seems like a century.

The entire hood can play ball,

But it's tradition to play

Street hustler and ball.

To many, this is our urban world normalcy.

We all pass the bottle of Ciroc with

Blurry visions while trying to envision-

Our passions in life.

Seeing a better future,

We're determined to become great men.

In the hood preachers shun our good

With stereotyped judgmental sins.

We thrive, trying not to deprive;

We want to fruitfully live and

Not vainly die.

We're not asking for handouts,

We are looking for opportunities

To exit out of these poverty-

Stricken hoods with death routes.

Our arms reach may seem short,

But it will not stop our persistence,

Or our hope towards for making it out.

We are optimistic about being beyond

More than No-good.

Our confidence aspires to the

Discovery of a greater life.

We have dreams that live

Beyond the street lights.

We have tough minds and tough hearts

That beat with successful might.

We vent, repent and keep alive

Our faith beyond sight.

Nothing will hold back our ambition;

Understanding where we are

Yet living for where we are going.

Chapter 38

Same Reality

Realistic situations relates circumstances;

Actualities knows casualties;

Different life, same tragedies.

Doesn't have to be in your city-

The same A.K sounds show no pity.

Identical white powder slanged through the streets;

Another child with nothing to eat.

The very same Ben-Frank transacted on

The street gives another child something to eat.

A teenage mother in the club on ecstasy;

She's only sixteen and her child one.

For sport, police bullets crucify

Our black and Hispanic teens;

It's an everyday standard routine.

Furniture on the curb from home evictions;

And another county jail admission.

The homie blasted two adversaries;

One died the other was paralyzed.

Another youngster with a life conviction.

No difference between your hood and mine;

We're pouring out liquor too...

For the homies we miss.

Respect the flag color-code with

The same expected towards your color-code.

Our livelihood esteems in the same manner;

With similarities in our shades of black,

We hanging the same way- where you at?

Inhaling Kush smoke or pistol smoke'

Both will get you high enough to choke.

Everyone's living to die!

It's a traditional reality for mothers to cry.

There's many suggestions with

No accurate opportunities;

With the same crooked seed planted

Within all inner city black communities.

It's a struggle for a black man to

Climb out his living grave;

Due to being buried alive, living life dead.

As black men we undergo same actualities;

But we're never weak men,

We are stronger than any sin.

We can overtake struggle and

Inspire our lives to be great men.

We have dodged bullets and

Can dodge prison plantations.

We can strategize to feed our families,

Acquire education and travel the world.

Black men, we win when we escape

Our daily devastation.

Chapter 39

Making a Change of Nonsense

Forevermore, MR.BIGMANN Grier will be

Reputable of creating responsible,

Intelligent peers successfully!

Loving our culture and creating

Intelligent and successful homies!

For our at-risk youth are in need of

Making a change of nonsense!

Living a positive life brings tranquility;

Having a peaceful flexibility in life

Brings a prosperous ability.

Therefore, be a chameleon with

Wholehearted optimism.

Being prejudice of Red, blue and black

Is a successive setback.

Your life's purpose won't win with pessimism;

Have the courtesy of effective endurance intact.

We all are brothers

Living out our destiny in success!

A positive attitude empowers-

Growth and development;

We'll forever be men

Apprehending future intelligence, always!

For our culture's awareness has courage.

Making a change of nonsense-

Is to be courageous!

For I will never turn my back on our youngsters;

That wouldn't be of noble common sense.

For if I do, may the real streets rebuke me,

And my God-hood forsake me.

For I am an O.G who

Was molded to positively think!

Now I reality-inspire the youngsters.

Making a change of nonsense.

Encourage the young and beyond

To set positive life goals.

The fear of not succeeding be not in our control;

Life is to be lived aiming to achieve.

There is value in keeping positive ambition.

To conceive your dreams is to believe;

With disciplined motives you will receive!

Chapter 40

Concerned Not

Who is concerned about the hailing tears?

Ran smears the cries of our world;

Senseless wars are the truest crimes.

Injustice is a game played to

Profit from men being penally confined.

The people's minds are being robbed blind.

Lies are accepted and not discerned;

Are we a nation of people wholly closed-minded?

Every season begets for a reason;

So there is a creative reason behind every problem.

A problem is first created,

Only to be strategically solved.

Who is truly concerned about solutions?

What is the real reason behind all four seasons?

Summer falls into winter,

So that spring can blossom into summer.

The evolution of life and death is

Unraveled before our daily seeing eyes.

Thus, some must die for majority to live.

Who is really concerned about whom lives?

Are we not concerned of the reasons people die?

Love is an emotional sense people share;

So it makes no sense not to love.

Love ourselves enough to love another;

Just as the day loves night so to share the sky.

Are we that hateful within our hearts?

To be always concerned not?

Chapter 41

We Need a Piece of Peace

We can sing Amazing Grace,

While lives are being

Bruised, misused and confused.

Did MR. BIGMANN Grier have to be sentenced

To life in order to be born again?

Did it require for his life

To be persecuted by unjust sins?

In order to get his life to exit sins

By exiting the pen.

The reality-truth asks,

Has MR. BIGMANN Grier truly won?

Winning back his freedom again…

When his mother addresses her son,

She tells of his cousin's sentence to 50 years.

To have a piece of justice seems a sin…

Peace is love;

Love conquers hate.

Just a piece of peace will invigorate.

Invigorate mankind from its violent fate;

If man loved himself and the world as one,

A piece of peace will live in the world today.

Peace cries for peaceful love;

Yet the world refuses peace a piece of love.

Do we even understand the battles of life?

When we ask for peace a piece of war detest;

Peace is a joy we profess.

Peace is a piece our life must address.

Peace is love;

Love conquers hate.

Just a piece of peace will invigorate.

Invigorate mankind from its violent fate;

If man loved himself and the world as one,

A piece of peace will live in the world today.

MR. BIGMANN Grier forgets not his days of old.

When his post traumatic gangbang

Nightmares chase his successful dreams.

It's crazy sleeping with one eye open

Watching over my now righteous soul.

It is evident God is my protected armor;

Yet it feels lonely without a nickel plated piece;

To keep my zone in peace.

MR. BIGMANN Grier prays to keep his mind,

Heart and soul at peace.

Life is always calling to death for peace;

If only living could let life live in peace.

Only then the world can have a piece of peace.

Peace is love and love conquers hate.

Just a piece of peace will invigorate.

Invigorate mankind from its violent fate;

If man loved himself and the world as one,

A piece of peace will live in the world today.

Chapter 42

The Pinnacle of a Man

The culmination of a man is to exert internal peace.

The warrior like energy of a man is to

Exercise, fortify and prosperously increase.

MR. BIGMANN Grier knows sin as a past friend;

From experiences of being a dangerous man.

Growth in life is not living in vain;

For there are those men still stagnant,

Not productively growing in life.

Beware of fraudulent men's claims;

For they emulate who they are not.

Being in favor of fake orientations

Will bring your life blind pain.

Hope conveys truth to reality despite

The breath of life being withdrawn by casualties.

Will an authentic man hate?

The question can be answered through love;

RealityPoetry Ark of Inspirational Wisdom
MR. BIGMANN GRIER

Invigorated poetically for many men to relate.

To live a lie is to despise truth!

The biggest secret in the world is

Hidden within every man's heartbeat.

Where ever a real man dwells-

In the depths of the real streets,

In a caged prison cell or among the suits on Wall St.

The potential to overcome will always be

Submitted by the actuality dwelled.

The totality of a man's life is fit

For a successful paradise not a poor hell.

Thought the serpentines deceive still-

We must overpower a devious torment

In order to escape the

Afflictions of life's devastations.

Real men defeat all that will attempt

To stress their life!

The pinnacle of a man is to conquer self!

The process of self-actualization brings

Wholeness with each emancipated heartbeat felt.

Chapter 43

RealityEssay: Victory Over Anger

Anger is a strong feeling of intense injustice towards yourself, those important to you and all who you encounter. Anger is full of displeased emotions and hate. Hate that empowers forward bitterness within your heart; causing an angry rejection of living within the harmony of happiness. Anger's attitude ridicules and keeps your life from a joyous peace.

An angry individual is quick to acknowledge another's anger while denying the anger they have housed within themselves. He who will not acknowledge his own anger slowly mentally kills themselves. Attitude defines character; anger I an expression of an individual's characteristics. With anger, a lack of self-love leads to a numbing of the emotions to love and be loved. Anger confuses emotions. Living within a drowning of angry emotions leads to a resistance to evolve. Succumbing to anger will bring loneliness to your life. Do not live to die alone! For anger is a danger to your wellbeing.

Love does not love anger. Love is confronted with anger when anger dwells within. Anger will hinder love from entering the heart's front door; even by self-inflicted anger. Lack of peace, self-control and kindness indwelling within you results from that same anger. Frustrations, stress and anguished emotions are the winners of an angry heart. An angry heart affects health and its hostility manipulates to misery. With that love will eventually exit the back door of your life.

Victory over anger begins when you identify your anger. If your past burdens are living as present internal burdens, you may be actuating external problems in your life. This living anger within your heart must be resolved; if not it will affect your future life experiences. You must overcome anger and bitterness. Releasing your anger will awaken peace within yourself. Peace will illuminate the mind and heart.

Be willing to confess your anger openly to your God and anyone else who loves you so to help rid you of that anger. Do not reject their love and support. Rejecting the peace of love that comes from the help will only suffocate your emotions and perpetuate more anxiety. Anger makes you indecisive, stressing your sane decisions. Being honest with yourself and identifying your anger will help you to relieve that anger.

If you do not rid yourself of anger you will lose all who are within your life. No one is receptive to an angry attitude, bitterness, slander or rage. Your anger can congest others with turmoil and distract their road of happiness they are on. Happiness is a way of life and anger is a killer. The two can never conjoin in harmony. Manage, relieve and liberate your anger. Rid your anger victoriously by changing your self-inflicted anger into love. Love lives in peace!

Once visible, anger is a clear expression of who you are. Continuously have victory over your enemy- anger. Detach the angry root and replace with the root of love. Inhabit peace within your heart.

RealityPhorism Sage

The meaning of death is found in life and the meaning of life is found in death. Both coexists within each other. Life can't live void of death and death results from life. Avoid fear of life and death's existence. Live your life to the fullest. Do not let death acquire your life before you!

PART IV

SPIRITUAL-WISDOM

Chapter 44

Faith

The power of Faith manifests all that is prayed for; the key to all doors in life is Faith. Without Faith, nothing prayed for will come to be. Faith has to be the most powerful word God has given us. With Faith, God created the world and created us, the people. We, his creation can employ Faith. Unlike other creatures who operate solely through nature, people utilize Faith to bring to fruition all our life's desires. The power of our Faith strengthens us to produce that which our life calls for. He who thinks little, receives little; he who thinks great receives greatness. Faith is the drive behind each thought. Keep the Faith by being faithful to it. Forever stay strong in your Faith and blessings will Faithfully befall you!

Chapter 45

Rise to Glory

For I live within an allegiance of Godly love;

It is my rock, umbrella, and armor.

I faithfully arise through the storm,

The trials, the persecution and the war.

My strength couldn't bear the pain on its own;

Without God's strong hand on my increase.

Despite all the long suffering pessimism

I've optimistically ascended into a great man.

My history has its portion of negative sins,

But my rise acknowledges gloriously a positive begin.

My honor will be applauded righteously;

My pureness assailed impurities to descend.

This is evidence of a man's faith being his friend;

Rooted within his eternal believing heart.

Captivity in a one man cell,

With 24 hour lockdown,

Persistent creativity couldn't be held down.

Mind expanding emancipation soared

With my poetic thoughts;

Knowing only death could hold me down.

My freedom's breath is a fact-

MR. BIGMANN Grier is coming home!

My heart beats exalted success;

Void of congested, doubtful stress.

I am gloriously empowered;

Through God's plan that has

Been manifested and blessed!

Chapter 46

Fathom Essence

Understand the parable of

MR. BIGMAN Grier's quintessence reality.

Identify with a man unjustly condemned;

Who sheds impurities that beget his purest whole.

For his heart wed his faith as

He matured in his lonesomeness.

There's no sunshine in high max;

Yet he envisions the sun shining wholesome.

Ponder the molding of a dead man born again

With life, coming alive.

Memories of yesterday's adversity is

The strength motivating todays thrive.

Look into the mind of

One that has conquered an artistic genius;

For his future opulence isn't blind.

To see the light- read between the lines!

He became blessedly inclined.

His empowering sense for wise inspiration

Is his change in his life dedication.

A will for emancipation gave understanding;

Severing his ties with behaviors that fed

Into the world's devastation.

This poetic parable is wisdom of reality;

From a man discerning an

Essential spiritual realization.

Chapter 47

Abundant Increase

An act of God blessed MR. BIGMANN Grier

With an aspiration for an abundant, affluent life.

Daily activity developed a *financializing* plot,

From financial literacy and drafting a lot.

An abundant blue print was outlined,

With enactments of business savvy.

An affluent picture envisioned,

Within an opulent realistic frame.

Progress and increase unfold mega sums of riches;

Poor excuses get excused.

My increase comes of a financial,

Intelligent development.

An abundancy of planning ahead

Expands my life's full value!

From currency advancing among legal tender,

There is no more illegal funds conspired.

Banks now transact my cash through the wire!

MR. BIGMANN Grier shows great

Generosity towards the people.

For he will aid an economy increase.

Being modest with contrived capital is

The creative creation of a giving heart.

Sharing a blessing of abundance is

The modeling of a generous heart.

My finance-wisdom will merge urban minds;

With a financial cultivating incline.

Life is meant to be lived enduring abundance,

Enriched by a financial education.

Chapter 48

Fear Not Sinning

For I am not a devil;

Although I've undergone sins with evil men.

I am now a divine man!

MR. BIGMANN Grier has a discernment of-

The maliciousness within hellish streets;

The riding high of adversaries,

As they creep sinisterly.

For beats pound deviously hard;

God reveals every heart isn't evil- hard.

Living begets a divine lesson,

We call upon God to help our life get better!

Evil and hate attempt to assassinate-

All the blessings prayed for.

Why do sins expect you not too faithfully thrive?

Bury your sinister drive;

One great prayer a day will bring faith alive.

Sinning is not a way to

Fuel life with a prosperity-drive.

Faith is the perseverance for

Submission to a purposeful journey.

Faith will see visions clear when you don't fear;

Fret not sinning, for nothing will fail thee,

When your faith knows-

What God has predestined thee!

Chapter 49

Street Gospel Truth

Street-religion truth breeds God-hood;

Glorifying a true religion.

Without sinister mindsets of men,

Life would be lived among praise of divine men.

Persecution resulted in prison for many great men;

MR. BIGMANN Grier, Malcolm X,

Martin Luther King, and Tupac Shakur.

Persecutors always fail to win;

Street gospels truth are reality sound bullets

Aiming towards an awakening from sin.

With more children being born everyday;

The breeding of chosen ones must never stop.

The real street knows who must watch the cops.

Trayvon Martin died innocently by

The gun of a neighborhood watch.

Why is it those that eye over our world

See and hear no evil?

We're told we are too evil to

Obtain blessings as God's people.

Designed lies has the youth living against all odds!

The gospel speaks the truth towards

Arising the life of our youth.

Chapter 50

Save YourSelf

If you have undergone a courageous walk through the wilderness...

If you have been the victim of long suffering...

If you have adhered to sinister actions...

You can liberate your life faithfully-

Recognizing the God within your spirit!

If you never knew- know that you are a God.

Save YourSelf by accepting the God in YourSelf.

You will then come to discern through faith

The reasons your sins had to die.

Save YourSelf by accepting YourSelf.

Don't undermine the God in you

By living within a sinful nature to get by.

Many fail to believe unfailingly in themselves;

Be the one to accept YourSelf unconditionally.

Never doubt YourSelf,

Love you!

Believe that the world loves you

As you love YourSelf.

Adore the Godly trio within your heart;

Trust, faith and belief in YourSelf.

When you love YourSelf it will never forsake you.

Trust in your inner self,

Have faith in YourSelf,

Accept YourSelf as God.

In this natural life endure Godly favor.

Walk in faith with all your might;

For it will be the greatest love of your life.

All for a simple fee of trust and belief.

Save YourSelf by accepting YourSelf.

Achieve a purposeful, righteous life.

Save YourSelf by accepting YourSelf!

Chapter 51

Heavens Written

MR. BIGMANN Grier's fate was heaven sent...

I endure through life walking faithfully in tune with my spirit. I live anointed and strong as David, wise and abundant as Solomon. If someone had said to me that a pen would become my greatest weapon I would have called them a liar! I have now come to realize that our strengths are the attributes we never give the greatest attention to; "A Man's gift makes room for him and brings him before great men" (Pro.18:16). We undergo trials in our lives by choices and predestined fate. It is on us as to how successful are our victories and whether we undergo suffering or joy. Whether good or bad, everything is a test; a test of whether we will make the righteous choice or not. Everyone has a testimony in life. As it is written in one of the world's most recognized books, inscribed old to new are blessed inspirations. Faithfully, I have come to witness what faith and belief can do in our lives. When we act out in faith, trust and belief we are free in heart and mind. With overstanding of this, all things desired will come to be. I am grateful of blessings and am renewed everyday. Life is what we make it; we cannot blame anyone for the circumstances that befall us. We must have understanding of life situations and not point a finger. Become a greater person; inspirit God within your life experiences. God is within us and never leaves us. Call upon faith and bring to you true peace of mind, peace of heart and fruitful blessings to your life. Life Is what you make it! Live it faithfully and it will become more alive and things will change for the greater of you. I, MR. BIGMANN Grier am a witness; my life has changed for the greater of myself and my purpose- and that's heavenly written!

Chapter 52

Servant Leadership

(Christ-like)

A wise servant leader inspires and fortifies the world. MR. BIGMANN Grier concurs that servant leadership is harmonious with Jesus Christ. The story of Jesus reign manifested his servitude and leadership. Jesus served the people with a new revelation of God's love and encouraged people out of sin. He did so by way of great compassionate service of his leadership. Servant leadership is a utilization of Jesus actions. The servant leadership employed by Robert Greenleaf's virtues emulate healing, empathy, stewardship, and awareness. The characteristics mirror the attributes of Jesus in whole.

Foresight is another attribute of a servant leadership vision. A vision which has become futuristic from the present's eye. Jesus foretold realities of our present through foresight of servant leadership. Jesus forewarned his disciples of reincarnation even as they doubted his words. Jesus behavior was shaped from servant leadership when offering understanding of lessons from Moses era. His reincarnation was to make truth of what he foretold; so to know that God Prevails!

An individual must first understand his perception of self-awareness. An awareness can be strengthened with understanding. An ability to enable motivates a self-awareness drive and regenerates solace in others. An emotional intelligence manages empathy and a servant leader begets a servicing leadership of committing to the growth of people. Servant leadership is a whole of principles, attributively Christ-like.

Chapter 53

God's Aim

Looking out amongst the world-

I see God's people!

Even if you do not talk or look like me,

We are all God's people;

We are all equal.

The return of Christ is a sequel;

So we must not follow our flesh,

It is already amongst the dead.

Always walk in spirit and

Faith will keep your from being misled.

The more spiritually attune you are-

The more you will discover yourself.

This is a true unification with God.

We follow our inner emotions and

Neglect the will of our inner spirit notions.

Focus your emotions and motives to

Live solely for God;

He will put us in situations so

We can come to deny ourselves and

Open a blind spiritual eye to see him!

As God's people we must

Know faithfully God is just,

And relive ourselves of unjustified faults.

Understanding God's justice will never come late;

Impatience never believes in God's fate.

Trust that God's justice will make its date!

As God's aim is-

You must rely on him in all matters;

Your selfish desires you must shatter!

Believe and pursue God as you

Take action towards living your life.

In this natural life, MR. BIIGMANN Grier

Is undergoing a spiritual aim of God;

This *realitypoem* is truth of spirituality.

For this is far from a miracle;

It is all an inner spirit discovery of evidence

When one is in tune with the realm of-

Their inner spirit residence!

Chapter 54

God's Time Possesses Man's Time

God's time is not on man's time;

No man knows God's time;

God is always on time-on God's time;

Man's time comes late sometimes;

Yet can be early at times.

Man's time, at times comes on time.

Yet, all the time-

God's time is accurate time!

Man's time may give up on God's time;

God's time never gives up on revealing man's time.

God's time manifests man's time.

When God's time anoints blessings upon man's time

Those are forever good times.

Patient timing strengthens faith in time.

Time management grants man the

Time to prepare himself for God's time.

Be careful not to waste your time;

Nor let another man distract your time.

God's time wastes no time;

Remember you do have the time when

You're attuned to God's time;

For God's time knows man's time.

**RealityPhorism Sage:*

Time doesn't exist within man's time; it is a mere illusion upon man's time. One must set the time within. God's time is within all time!

Chapter 55

Man of God

Scientist (man) fail to understand an event of night that turned day into our creation; as God molded man. It is speculated that powerful forces are responsible for erasing the first DNA of life beginning on earth. God has not allowed man to fully tamper with his creation; for no evidence of the first DNA of life has ever been discovered, and never will be. God will never reveal his secret. God doesn't desire man to know the blueprint of how he created life; God is not of science but of faith. The faith of God is an existence, that from which man was created. A master would never bestow his every thought into a mind that he created; for man is already endowed with an ability to think accordingly, as God. Man can only theorize as to how God's creation came to be; for no test nor experiment leaves a pure answer for how man came to be. Yet, Scientists (man) will convolute a theory in his mind as if he can undermine God's universal doctrine of creation. Man always finds himself with ponders and wonders, theories not facts, his own concluding thoughts- not evidence of facts. Without a proven theory, man can dwell in the realm of prayer (meditation) and find more of himself. Man's mere presence is evidence of God's existence whether you believe in a higher power or not. The abundance of man in today's world and his ability to think and intelligently create is evidence that God exists. More and more man has become accepting of spirituality. The grace of spirituality allows one to accomplish in life with everlasting joy and happiness. Spirituality lives within man. MR. BIGMANN Grier advises every man to grasp the spiritual energy within himself; with realization that God is great-spirit and Man is of God!

Chapter 56

God's Government

This is a government built on sharing beliefs;

A moral framework signifying the meaning of peace.

The church is not a building,

It is the people- with God built within them.

This doesn't necessarily exclude sin;

Frustrated, we may still take a sip of the gin.

When prayer goes up blessings come down;

A continuous fight, round after round.

This government isn't run by the president;

But by the laws of the land which are evident.

Knowing that this natural order is heaven sent.

God's government is established for his children;

For he is our father and we are his pilgrims.

The lust of this world desires furs and diamond rings;

I pray and hope God sees me through for

I know God's government is truly true.

I pray for divine sight so to see

Past the wicked desires of evil hearts,

And false bravery.

**Excerpt from "The Art of ConsciousPoetry: Physical, Mental & Spiritual" By ConsciousPoet: KaKa Hunta, 2013*

Chapter 57

RealityEssay:

MR. BIGMANN Grier's Mind Theory

"Thinking beyond deep is evidence one's mind never sleeps. I understand that the mind possesses infinite intelligence and we must be in tune and grasp that intelligence within the mind."

February 27, 2008

5:43 PM

For the mind is not a product of the brain; the brain is a product of the mind. The brain can be held, touched and seen in physical form; yet the mind is invisible, visible only within the realm it resides. The brain being a provider of human life, the mind is its strength. Take a dream for instance... in a dream perceives people they have never encountered before. One does not consciously draw up a diagram of what they will encounter yet it comes about from mind's peace during sleep. Those who share a frequency mind wave, a balance, a warping of the minds while asleep, channel the minds to encounter. Consider a person who is in a coma... Although in a physical coma, internally they may be alive; with their mind in a zone just not having found a way back to reality yet. An individual who was in a coma for three months revealed to me that the sound of his mother's voice over a phone induced a movement from him. In theory, being in a coma you are a step away from death, yet you are dealing with your inner self. People may talk to you and all though you can't respond your ears hear. The mere voice of his mother over the phone brought him out of unconsciousness, although he had been conscious within his mind enough so that he responded with physical movement. The sound of his loved ones voice brought him back into the existence of his external self. *(Referenced coma patient: Antwan "Lil-Outlaw" Lockett)*

The mind is so powerful it thinks without letting one know. The mind builds intelligence without asking the body, it just do so. The mind is the spirit of life itself! The mind is power and knowledge of self; being in tune with your mind gives you greater power of self. The mind will conceive a thought and the brain will flex that thought into existence with one's external self. A mind never forgets a thought; it can consume galaxies for it is a universe of its own.

February 28, 2008

9:30 PM

The mind exists within the brain; it breathes life into the existence of the brain. Although you can't have surgery on the brain and reveal the mind, the mind is what keeps the brain alive; just as the body can't function without internal breath. The two function together. The mind makes the brain come to life. The mind in itself is a spirit that just is!

RealityPhorism Sage

God's investment... Spirit is God's investment within you. Acknowledging this investment within your inner self will bring you infinite fruit. Your spiritual energy is an abundance of all things; all things will faithfully derive from your inner self. Invest time within your inner spirit and your external-self shall excel!

RealityPhorism Sage

Your choices become your circumstance; life is the result of the choices we make. That which you think and provide is what will mold whatever circumstances you beget. You are in control of what will take course...within the greatness of freewill.

PART V

LOVE-WISDOM

Chapter 58

Love's Epigram

Love is not a noun;

Not a person, place or thing.

Love is more of a verb;

To feel love- love must be alive!

Although, one can love a

Person, place or thing;

Love doesn't reside within

No place or thing.

Love resides within a person;

A person who can exert love.

A place can be loved,

But cannot love.

A thing can be loved,

But cannot love.

Love's actions are experienced;

By a person-pervading from a person!

Chapter 59

Elements of Love

Love is an affectionate fulfillment.

Water is a thirst quencher for dried love.

Fire is the burning desire of a loving heart.

Diamonds and gems are an awe of love.

Peace is the victory of love.

Friendships are an enthusiasm of love;

Bonded and interdependent of love.

Marriage is the sacredness of love.

Commitment is the vow of love and

Fidelity is its fruitfulness.

Understanding is the communication of love.

Trust is the strength of love.

Pleasing is the fellowship of love.

Wine is a delicate taste of love.

Sex is an inspiration of love.

Gracefulness is of genuine love as

Happiness is an abundance of love.

A lifetime is the journey of love.

Only love can feed love...

Chapter 60

Lovelies Lied to Love

Lies are fake impressions;

When a liar love appears as an authentic expression.

Lovelies is a heart professing

Unrealistic love confessions!

Lies to love strengthens any relationship to depart;

A heart that loves won't accept-

False love conversing lies!

No matter the depth of love,

Love doesn't desire to be blinded by a love lie!

Tears within the eyes of lies

Come not from a devoted love,

But solely a cry of another love-lie.

Love desires veracity, not a liar's pity!

The testimony of unconditional love

Will never commit perjured affection,

Not within a loving heart!

Loves rapture doesn't conamore passion;

For love-lies glorified fiction.

No woman or man deserves love-lies friction;

Whether within a marriage or friendly love devotion.

An adoring rapport one shares should

Always be an enchantment.

The beauty of loving doesn't admire ugly deception;

For love must be appreciated,

With passionate perception.

Lies to love makes loving become numb

Within the heart of a love loving.

An unfailing love never lies;

Undying love despise lies;

True love will never lie!

When love-lies lie to love-

Love's respect lies brokenhearted.

Chapter 61

Love and The Poet

Love's affectionate emotions are-

Feelings to admiringly characterize!

Love allures the *RealityPoetry* within

The poet to passionately create.

The poet's artistic genius entitles-

Love glory as caring!

Love's wisdom- the poet will forever idolize!

Love soothes hearts;

Valuing love as a fond prize.

The ideal of love thoughtfully

Opens the poet's mind-eye.

The poet's heart amorously makes passionate love;

To love, kissing creatively!

The poet is distinguishes love's

Beauty as an attentive attraction,

Transcribing an infatuation for love's appeal.

The poet recites a love poem within the

Heart of love, while making skillful love!

The poet narrates lovely designs;

Describing love-round breast and

Love-hard elongated nipples.

The poet explicitly poeticizes love;

Romantically caressing love's warm and moist vulva.

The poet embraces love poetically;

Love anxiously clasps the poet.

Love adores the poet!

The poet gently crafts love's curves,

Artistically capturing love's thighs.

Love charms the poet with

Love's possessive crush.

The poet's devotion to love begets

From love's tender touch.

The poet's *RealityPoetry* offers

Love a genuine, passionate thrust!

Chapter 62

Red & Blue Roses

Red roses signify love;

Blue roses express loyalty.

Red roses of love,

Blue roses of loyalty,

The red rose is because I love you!

The blue rose is because I am loyal!

Loyal to the love and loyalty we share-

Red roses for our love!

Blue roses for our loyalty!

My love, here is your red rose;

Love faithfully, adoring this red rose.

Faithfully love, trusting with this blue rose.

Red and blue roses blossom

When devoted and obedient.

Love and loyalty is the root of our passionate bonds;

Passionate red roses of love;

Bonded blue roses of loyalty.

Red & Blue roses are loyalty, love and rosy!

Chapter 63

Love's Sacred Passion

Compassion makes you call an enemy a friend.

Dispassion makes you bitter,

Bitter to yourself and friends.

Love's sacred passion invigorates-

Your heart's purest passion;

A passion that devours dispassion!

A loving passion will extend a kind passion;

This is an essence of love-

Loyal sacred passion!

How can one love himself with a sacred passion?

Love is not sacred unless the

Strength of your love's passion is-

Sacredly loving someone else.

Love's passion disheartens any heart's hate;

Love's passion overpowers all anger's fate.

Loyalty is a passion many can't render;

For one can only be loyal when

One passionately trust themselves to love tender.

It is great to have one passionate heartbeat,

Instead of a heart pounding numerously with

The drive of love's deceit.

Love's passion is durable when

Loyalty to love is passionately deep.

Loyal passion is strong when

Love and loyalty are passionately complete.

Chapter 64

Forbidden Love

The juice of forbidden fruit

Opens mankind's eyes to sin.

Forbidden love osculates lust that

Unpleasantly rapports love's end-

Prohibiting your love to be trusted,

By tasting another outside your love;

Forbidding love to be genuine!

Who can you blame for this unfaithful love shame?

Flirting intimately, forgetting

The ethics of love's name.

True love doesn't conceive pain;

Immorality extracts unconditional love's fame.

To promiscuously extort love is a consummate game.

Disloyalty is the reason many forbid love's name!

Find undying love to love you;

Find it with whom unfailingly loves himself.

Who would forbid love to oneself?

Your love will be cherished,

As you are one with them.

The answer to love's reign is

Love enjoying love without pain.

Chapter 65

Worthy

Are you worthy of love?

Worthy of a love wooing...

Are you worthy to be loved?

A love to wholeheartedly worship...

Wretchedness is a love unworthy;

And wrathful love has no worth.

Stay away from love unworthy;

Pain rains hail on summer's love.

A fruitful taste of love is a

Sweetening worth of love.

Fighting makes love worthless;

Loves not worthy of battered hate.

Love's value is worth more than gold.

Admire whoever you love;

Don't turn your love with scold.

Warm-hearted loving keeps

Your love from getting cold.

Honoring love is bold,

Heartfelt and worthwhile.

Worthy love always lasts;

Appreciate it with a worthy smile.

We are all worth the worthwhile

Of a love divine.

Every man and woman desires a

Love worth loving unblind.

Moral love keeps your heartrate loving kind.

Good-for-nothing love is unworthy;

Dependable love is grand and trustworthy.

Be a worthy man or woman worthwhile to love.

Chapter 66

Loving to Love

Loving to love is a refreshing feeling;

For love itself knows truelove;

For love bears value;

For knowing how to love is a great sensation;

Loving to love-

Will teach you how to wholeheartedly love.

For love nourishes love-

To love thyself with love.

For even God's love invigorates your heart to love;

For it is evident love is yours to love!

For love is worthy of all your love!

The love you share is sacred love.

Love will always love;

For your serenity glistens love;

For being peaceful polishes love;

For discernment honors love;

With confidence in love.

Do you truly love to love?

Always love yourself as you love others!

Chapter 67

Perfect Man meets Perfect Woman

When an ideal man meets an ideal woman-

The fulfillment of immaculateness

Has completed an ideal brand.

When the perfect somebody is met-

An embodiment of perfection develops,

A bond spiritually formed.

The perfect man's eyes will not only look,

But see the happiness within their future.

When the perfect woman speaks,

The man will not only hear her voice,

He will listen to her entire loving heart as

It beats impeccably through her voice.

When the perfection of their love mates

Passionately between the sheets;

Their souls will ecstatically mate, perfectly.

As a flawless diamond,

Their wholeness of love is-

An extraordinary perfection.

The perfect man meets the perfect woman,

When he embraces her imperfection;

As the perfect woman accepts faults of her man.

The perfect man will appreciate his perfect woman;

She will understand her man.

Neither will abuse their mutual perfection.

Their completeness has no secrecy and never lies;

The perfect couple keeps perfect love alive.

Chapter 68

Love & Loyalty

"Love is the bond between you and another. Loyalty is to keep anything from coming in between that bond".

It took God's love to create you;

Your parents made love to conceive you;

Loyalty is unspoken protection;

Loyalty has no need for correction;

Love is guided by the heart;

Love is not love without the whole;

Loyalty from the mind is not smart;

Loyalty is guided by the love within heart;

When love does not exist-

Loyalty has no allegiance within the people;

Love's activeness keeps loyalty alive;

Love and loyalty fortifies all.

PART VI

POSITIVE-WISDOM

Chapter 69

Believe

Fate and faith conceive a destiny to be confident;

Believe!

Whatever you think about you can bring about.

Forget doubt and all negative people-shout!

Believe!

You can progress from what has you down and out!

Life is a journey with many routes;

Believe!

The hardest step is the first, don't give up

Especially when you've already begun to achieve;

Believe!

When you dream it becomes your reality;

Only you can make it your reality!

Dreams do come true, it is all about you;

Believe!

All is possible with persistence;

Nothing of the world is impossible with consistency;

Believe!

All things of this world is for you;

All you have to do is proceed with effort and

Believe!

Chapter 70

Smile

Take a serious look into your own eyes and smile!

Let your teeth glow and smile!

Forget cries of headaches and hardships and smile!

Feel a smooth melody as your heartbeats joyously slow and smile!

Give yourself a pat on the back, no matter where you're at and smile!

Listen to your favorite song while on the go and smile!

Do not think less of yourself; thank yourself for doing your best and smile!

Enrich your fellow friend with positive aspirations from within and smile!

Relax your mind and relieve your stress and smile!

Gangsters, take that mean mug off your face; hate is not in your space when you smile!

Ladies, kiss your man with love; men give your lady more love- as love makes love, smile!

BlackMen greet your BlackWomen with respect;

BlackWomen acknowledge that your BlackMen have confidence and strength. BlackPower is not to be neglected, black interdependence has eternal length. Smile in the black together- smile!

Don't be selfish, call someone and tell them you love them. Make someone else smile so you can smile with them-Smile!

Chapter 71

The Truth Lies

If you tell your truth would it be considered a lie?

If you tell a lie would it be considered the truth?

For what use is the truth when the truth is a lie?

When lies are accepted as truth what is its use?

Wholehearted truth...

The truth within your eyes doesn't see a lie;

So the lie you cry has no tears of truth.

Don't you rather see the naked truth then hear a dressed up lie?

If you undress the lie will you see the truth?

Allow the truth to be told.

The truth is not a lie but a lie can be the truth.

Chapter 72

21st Century Black

Do you know who you are?

Don't define yourself by the minority stereotype,

When you're the majority world hype.

You've been duplicated for years;

The story is designed to negatively give you fears-

Fears of your own self,

Fears of your peers,

Fears of your health,

Fears that you'll die on your 21st year,

Fears that you're too poor to pursue wealth.

Well think again my peers-

You have the mind to think my friend;

Think of yourself beyond a sin.

Nevertheless, a BlackMan of moral character;

With the personal initiative to win-

Not just in sports and music;

Likewise, in education, entrepreneurship and faith.

BlackMen, we are not that project that is projected!

Therefore, use your creative brain,

Express those neglected prodigy thoughts.

When we fail to define ourselves we

Grant the projection of others to define us!

You're not the definition of adversity complete;

Everything about you isn't street.

It's cool to be your true self;

You're real when you actually know yourself!

Don't define all your money resources as

Gun, robberies and cocaine resources.

For what about those ideas you have?

Tupac Shakur said it encouragingly,

Use your brain!

We are who we make ourselves to be!

This isn't the 19th century;

We are undergoing the cultivating 21st century.

For you and me there is an opportunity; we have to seek and we will find.

Don't give up if not accepted the first time!

We're to successively strong to bow down,

And too purposefully hard to fold.

Continue with a positive mental attitude.

You and I know Mama didn't raise no fool;

Daddy said "always keep your cool".

Challenge yourself studying books

And in servitude to school;

You don't have to be sitting in a room,

Majority are in front of a computer.

The information age set a stage;

Let me tell you the truth-

Never believe in excuses,

For that would be procrasti-faking.

We are the BlackMen we choose to be!

Let us be the best BlackMen we can be!

Chapter 73

The Eyes of Wisdom and
The Mind of Knowledge

Wisdom is applied effectively

When its actions are felt.

Therefore, the pursuit of one's life is balanced

When their responsibilities of fulfillment are kept.

Thus, an end doesn't justify the means;

We as people have imperfect means.

The truth may hurt when it's truthfully spoken;

Yet still it is better than a lie that

Solely deceives ones faith!

Positive thoughts defeat negative hate;

Negativity is a bruise to positive fate.

Conceive a mind with knowledge to prevail;

For being educated with life goals is

The benefit to help you excel.

Understand the direction your life is obtaining;

To stagnate your progress isn't maintaining.

When your life compliments you with success

You thank God and never complain,

Even when things seem hard.

The harder the struggle,

The more you strengthen your odds.

From the eyes of wisdom

You can see your vision clear.

With a mind of knowledge you can

Achieve in life without fear.

Chapter 74

Opportunity is Knocking

Knock! Knock!

"Get away from my door"

Knock! Knock!

"What do you want?"

Knock! Knock!

Silence...

Never be afraid of an opportunity;

Answer the door for an opportunity.

Opportunities open doors in life.

When an opportunity is knocking

Be ready to let it in.

Creating opportunities will open your doors;

It will also help others to come in.

Preparing for an opportunity is how you win!

Chapter 75

The Faith in His Vision

They thought it would never happen;

Yet, the world viewed the

Inauguration of President Obama.

To have faith is to never say never;

The truth told-

America finally slayed Osama!

How should one feel

Growing up to be put down?

Due to his actions being systematic

To his *Urbanhood.*

The gestures of negation-

"Boy you're no good"

"You'll never be more than nothing" was the sound.

How could his dreams to success be found?

The heart of a man that-

Beats *Gangsterism* profoundly.

Can't give in- won't give up!

He knows he can win;

Damn, it's a must he stay down;

One day he'll come up over this hill;

Defining his life through his realitypoetry.

To become wise he will devour his foolish will!

The world's rotation seems to

Make time easy to see;

When opposed with natural life-

How in the hell is living a time for he?

To sow your own wounds of life is

The healing of a scar.

He refuses to lose by faith;

His reality is more than real;

No pleading, God negotiated his life deal.

A man who could hate but

Give no such energy to his vision?

Look at the glistening in his eyes;

The man who is too strong to cry,

Whose life is dark as a prison hole,

Repentance of all his persecution

Helped him break the mold.

Praying for the forgiveness of his many sins

Relieved his gangster-soul.

Righteousness ordains the

Life he was destined to suffer;

Though faithfully succeed.

Walking out the gates of a false imprisonment

Into a healthy and wealthy life;

He didn't think twice;

It was God's fate for him to

Freely crack the safe.

Looking back, now he can breathe;

With faith in his vision he sees beyond the odds.

Miraculously he walks as his

Reality-proverbs feed the youth of

Those same wrathful nights;

The *gangsta* that can see a killing before it comes-

Transpired the mind that conceived

A hundred billion dollars;

The man who lives a life that

Envisions every beat of his heart.

To part ways with himself

Will beget his worst enemy;

For his loyalty is engraved within.

Empirical advantages changed his motives;

For his good-felon thoughts conceived-

His *mastermindful* visual thoughts.

Chapter 76

Prosperity Covenant

Developing a definitive purpose is the motivational efforts toward a successful destination.

Going the extra mile is to ride into a prosperous manifestation.

Using applied faith frontlines in life's lanes fast!

Budget your time and money; financial literacy will bring financial freedom.

Finances will forever last!

Build a positive mental attitude with a love to survive.

The lust to stay alive is the will in your righteous strive!

Cultivate creative visions thinking of prosperity, smiling from prosperous visions.

Control your attention; blessings come from believing you're blessed.

Think accurately; every life has its own living initiative.

Assemble an attractive personality; peace lives in the mind and heart that is proactive to life's negative quarrels.

Create personal initiative; those achieving at heart succeed by enforced self-disciplined morals.

Maintain a sound heath; let your dignity keep your life strong.

Let your integrity fortify living with self-respect as your discipline endures your self-control.

Prosperity, generosity, enthusiasm is your covenant-behold!

Chapter 77

No Sense Makes No Cents

The world has more time than money;

Yet, we still act as though-

We're running out of time;

Chasing a paper substance with no

Equivalency to money.

We've been suckered into counterfeit by

Historic faces imprinted on counterfeit.

What is stacking riches when they're insufficient?

A lot of minds on the materialistic,

All that have no benefit!

Should we blame the government for this or

Come to understand legal tender?

Our lives can overcome any stressful tender;

The lack of financial sense has the

World with no sum of cents.

Many are stagnate with liabilities,

Which are lie-abilities!

With non-efficient, long term gain abilities.

The lack of financial intelligence is-

An ignorance to where your money went.

Before your paycheck is sent

Your leftover earnings are already spent.

How can you invest in self-belligerence?

When your dollar isn't making you any cents.

A lack of financial independence is

What keeps you behind on your rent.

When inflation is taking course

Recognize your legal tender doesn't make cents.

Overstand this financial-reality poem;

For it does make sense.

Learn to invest in assets that gain interest.

It's worth more than saving money in a bank;

Money saved has less interest than money invested;

Money saved has a deficit of money spent.

Learn to keep your money working for you;

Not you working for the money.

Ever since the days of old,

Land and gold have been wealth;

Ask yourself why it is the most valuable?

Common sense, both have more value than cents;

Assets are what we all need to acquire-

To make sum cents!

When paper money stops circulating

Those with legal tender in banks, walls

And in a cash stash won't have any cents.

Those with assets will have profitable cents!

Even your house and cars are liabilities,

So don't rely on it.

You should never trust in net worth;

You're taxed before you gain any worth!

Educate your financial ignorance,

So that you can always gain financial benefits.

The lack of financial literacy will

Not make your mind any sense,

Nor your purse or wallet any cents!

Financial freedom may not be

Your life's greatest success;

Yet, it will give your life more

Options to progress!

Chapter 78

RealityEssay: Perceptions of Deceptions

The world rotates from actuated hoodwinks crafted by the evil eyes of deception; whose subreptions solicit urban communities as victims of failure- faulting their own misleading subversions incepted. Straight forward common sense that is perceived deceptive is integrity and dignity blinded from a moral vision. Deceit is an amoral insight of deception that disillusions perceptions from moral influence. .Nevertheless, mendacious creates a mirage that seems absolute; yet the disguised truth is an imaginary observation of deceptiveness. Individuals have learned of deception since the beginning of time. Deceptions determination is heartless and maintains no emotions within its duties. Deception may seem a reality; when in great character a deceptive heart possess no virtue. Perception can argue that trickery can be employed in good-will if employed to fathom discernment. However, treacherous objectives share no common ground with this fact discerned...

Chapter 79

Positive Response Formula

Life is less thought - more feelings. Feelings react from the thoughts; yet the thought creates the feeling. The feeling becomes your thoughts! Therefore, your feeling created your thought. Positively think about it... you'll feel the recipe!

Perception noted: Consider that you can explore a thought and not feel like it. You can't feel whatever is clever and not think about it.

RealityPhorism Sages

Imagine not that you can't; imagine everyday that you can".

RealityPhorism Sage

Becoming great IS the faith of Greatness.

RealityPhorism Sage

A man who doesn't know where every cent of his dollar is going does not have any financial sense. Financial literacy makes Cents!

RealityPhorism Sage

The world is a maze; made of many perceptions of deceptions. You will get lost attempting to figure out the world. Focus on figuring out where YOU will take your life in the world. Write your own history as you live it today. Your truth will be known from your perceptions; your history will not be a chronicled past-lie.

Sound Wisdom of Reality

Hopefully, the reality of wise words from the wisdom of *RealityPoetry* have inspired you.

Hopefully, you have accomplished with an optimistic sound invigorated within every wise free verse.

Hopefully, this enchanting gift of *RealityPoetry* has empowered you through an enjoyable and articulate converse.

Hopefully, this poetic Ark of MR. BIGMANN Grier's expressions of wisdom has influenced your aspirations.

Hopefully, this Ark of Inspirational Wisdom's resonance disclosed a miraculously rational philosophy.

MR. BIGMANN Grier's healthy and wise perceptions and his animated diction provide a poetic reality; prevailing life experiences in a fluent poetic story. Every eloquent verse is composed to encourage a focus for success to come alive!